ISLAMIC ART

Recognizing Geometric Ideas in Art

Janey Levy

PowerMath™

The Rosen Publishing Group's
PowerKids Press™
New York

Published in 2007 by The Rosen Publishing Group, Inc.
29 East 21st Street, New York, NY 10010

Book Design: Daniel Hosek

Photo Credits: Cover © Corbis; p. 5 © Jon Spaull/Corbis; p. 7 © Christine Osbourne/Corbis; p. 9 © Ralph A. Clevenger/Corbis; pp. 12 (A, B), 13, 15, 18, 19 © Gérard Degeorge/Corbis; pp. 12 (C, D), 16, 17 (bottom), 20, 21 © Arthur Thévenart/Corbis; p. 17 (top) © Peter Harholdt/Corbis.

Library of Congress Cataloging-in-Publication Data

Levy, Janey.
  Islamic art : recognizing geometric ideas in art / Janey Levy.
      p. cm. — (Math for the real world)
  Includes index.
  ISBN 1-4042-3364-4 (lib. bdg.)
  ISBN 1-4042-6081-1 (pbk.)
  6-pack ISBN 1-4042-6082-X
  1. Geometry—Juvenile literature. 2. Geometrical constructions in art—Juvenile literature. 3. Art, Islamic—Juvenile literature. I. Title. II. Series.
  QA445.5.L48 2006
  516—dc22
                              2005014296

Manufactured in the United States of America

Contents

Art of the Islamic World

The prophet Muhammad established the religion of Islam in the early A.D. 600s. Islam soon spread from Muhammad's city of Mecca in the area now known as Saudi Arabia. Within a century, it had spread as far west as Spain and as far east as southern Asia. Today, Muslims—the followers of Islam—can be found in countries around the world.

As Islam grew and spread, it developed its own distinctive style of art that is full of beauty, rich color, and complex design. The teachings of Muhammad encouraged the growth and high quality of Islamic art. According to Muhammad, "God is beautiful and loves beauty." Muhammad also said, "God likes that when you do anything, you do it excellently."

Islamic art has its own **visual** language, which is used everywhere in Islamic art—in manuscripts and on buildings, pottery, metalwork, and rugs. Calligraphy, or artistic writing, is one important element in the visual language of Islamic art. Muslims' respect for the written word of the Qur'an, the Islamic holy book, led them to raise writing to an art form in the very early days of Islam. Designs based on flowers and plant forms are another important element in Islamic art's visual language. Geometric designs constitute a third important element.

This photograph shows Muslim women walking past the Tomb of Ali in Mazar-e Sharif, Afghanistan. The tomb was built to honor Ali, who was Muhammad's son-in-law.

5

The Role of Geometry in Islamic Art

It may seem surprising that geometry should be one of the most important elements in an art form. However, for Muslims, geometry plays a vital role in art. It has its own special purpose and meaning.

Unity, order, and balance are the laws of creation in Islam. Geometry expresses the unity that is found within the **diversity** of nature. The same geometry that is found in a snowflake can also be found in a flower and a beehive. Geometry, in other words, represents the universal laws that create order and balance in nature. For Muslims, this order and balance in nature is a reflection of the order and balance that govern the spiritual world.

In Islamic art, the role of geometry is to help Muslims focus on the unity, order, and balance in nature and the spiritual world. Geometric forms create harmony in art that is meant to help Muslims actually live in harmony.

The geometric forms in Islamic art may seem quite complex at first. **Polygons** and stars with 6, 8, 10, or even 12 points commonly appear. Shapes **interlock** in complicated ways. However, even the most complex designs are mostly based on the circle, which is the primary symbol of unity in Islamic art.

Geometric designs and calligraphy, which can be seen at the top of this photograph, cover the Dome of the Rock. The Dome of the Rock, built in the late A.D. 600s, is a shrine constructed on a Muslim holy site in Jerusalem, Israel.

7

Circles, Polygons, and Stars

How can you create designs with polygons and stars by starting with a circle? Let's look at some **diagrams**. Figure 1 shows a **hexagon** (drawn in green) inside a circle. Inside the hexagon is a large 6-pointed star (in blue) made from 2 **equilateral triangles** that **intersect**. The center of the star is another hexagon (in purple). Inside this hexagon is another 6-pointed star (in red). The center of this star forms yet another hexagon (in orange). Another 6-pointed star (in yellow) is inside this hexagon, and once again the center of the star forms a hexagon (in light green). This pattern can go on and on, with smaller and smaller hexagons and stars.

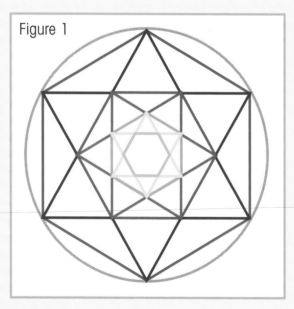

Figure 1

Why would Islamic artists be interested in hexagons? Hexagons are often found in nature, as we see in this honeycomb.

Figure 2 shows an **octagon** (in blue) inside a circle. Inside the octagon is an 8-pointed star (in purple) made from 2 **overlapping** squares. Just as the center of the 6-pointed star forms a hexagon, the center of the 8-pointed star forms an octagon (in red). Like the pattern in Figure 1, this pattern can go on and on, with smaller and smaller octagons and stars.

Figure 2

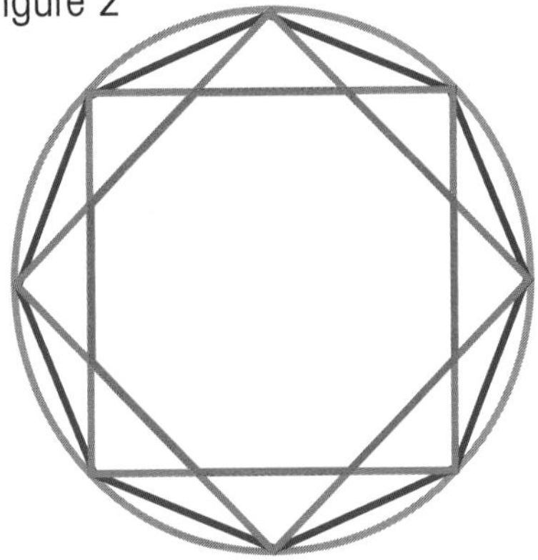

In Islamic art, the square was often a symbol for Earth. The 4 corners represent the 4 directions of the compass, or what were thought to be the 4 states of matter—solid, liquid, gas, and fire.

9

The points of the 8-pointed star in Figure 2 are short. An 8-pointed star with longer points can be made by extending the lines that form the sides of the squares, as shown in Figure 3. Notice that while the points of the 8-pointed star in Figure 2 are inside the circle, the points of this 8-pointed star extend outside the circle.

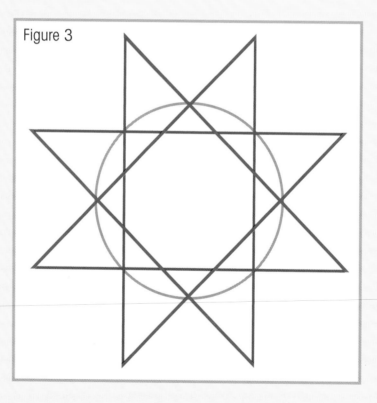

Figure 3

Overlapping circles can even be used to create a flower design, as shown in Figure 4. Here, 7 overlapping circles create a flower with 6 evenly spaced petals.

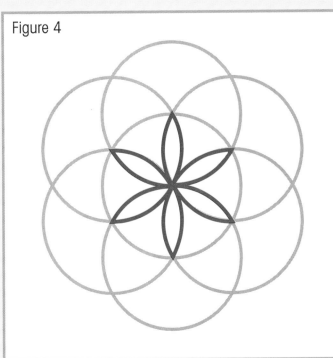

Figure 4

On the following pages, we'll look at some examples of these same designs that occur in Islamic art. You'll notice that circles aren't always visible in these designs. Just remember that they were the starting point for the artist even when we can't see them in the final artwork.

Some Islamic designs, like A and B, feature hexagons and 6-pointed stars.

Others, like C and D, feature octagons, 8-pointed stars with short points, and 8-pointed stars with extended points.

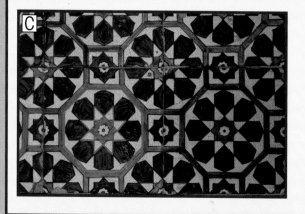

The example at the right features circles and the 6-petaled flowers created from overlapping circles.

There is room here to show only a few examples. However, even these few examples are enough to give some idea of the variety of forms that basic Islamic designs can take.

These designs all give visual form to fundamental Islamic beliefs. By starting with a circle—the symbol for unity—and creating a variety of complex, carefully structured geometric shapes, Islamic artists express the order and diversity found within the unity of nature.

This tilework decorates an Islamic building in Pakistan.

13

Symmetry, Patterns, and Tessellations

The geometric forms of Islamic art express the balance as well as the order of nature through their symmetry. Symmetry is the state of having the same size and shape on opposite sides of a dividing line or around a point or axis. Each of the geometric shapes we've looked at has symmetry. Circles, hexagons, octagons, and stars all have reflective or **bilateral** symmetry. This means that if you draw a straight line—known as a line of reflection—through the middle of the shape, each half is a mirror image of the other half.

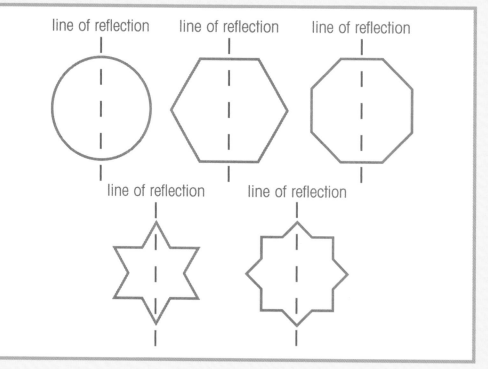

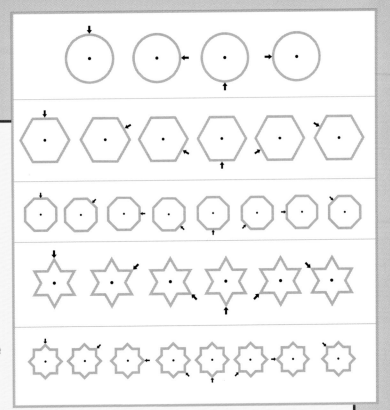

Each of the shapes to the right has rotational symmetry. This means that if you rotate each around its center, it will match the original shape and position more than once in a complete turn. The arrows next to each shape show the movement of the shape as it rotates around its center.

Each of the shapes above also has bilateral symmetry. However, the symmetry of Islamic art is not limited to individual shapes. In Islamic art, individual shapes are combined to form patterns that cover entire surfaces. These patterns also exhibit symmetry. Sometimes the patterns have bilateral symmetry, just as the shapes have.

 Each half of this tile pattern is a mirror image of the other half.

15

Bilateral symmetry is such an important principle in Islamic art that it occurs not just in geometric patterns, but also in designs based on flower and plant forms.

The tile decoration above comes from the Friday Mosque in Esfahan, Iran. The center portion is a complex geometric design centered on a 12-pointed star. It has both bilateral and rotational symmetry. The side panels have designs based on flower and plant forms. Each side panel has bilateral symmetry.

This antique rug from Iran has bilateral symmetry. The rug's colorful central design has both bilateral and rotational symmetry.

Symmetry in patterns in Islamic art also includes transformations. A symmetry transformation is the repetition of a shape or design by flipping it, turning it, or sliding it to a new position. A transformation is different from bilateral or rotational symmetry because it involves multiple copies of the same shape or design. Symmetry transformations are common in Islamic art.

The tilework below is from a tomb in Multan, Pakistan. It shows a transformation of an 8-pointed star design. Any way the star is flipped or moved would result in the same shape. You can also see examples of bilateral and rotational symmetry within the design.

Sometimes symmetry transformations are repeated endlessly in all directions, forming a tessellation. A tessellation is an arrangement of shapes on a surface so that they fit together perfectly without overlapping or leaving gaps. In many tessellations, the shapes meet to form a perfect fit around a **vertex**. The angles around a vertex add up to 360º, the same number of degrees in a circle.

Regular tessellations are made up of 1 kind of shape. Three shapes can be used to form regular tessellations: equilateral triangles, squares, and regular hexagons. Such tessellations are another way for Islamic artists to express the order and balance in nature.

In this tilework, regular hexagons create a regular tessellation. Note that while the hexagons repeat, the decoration on the hexagons varies. This is an expression of diversity within the unity and order of nature.

Semiregular tessellations are made up of units composed of 3 or more regular polygons that form a perfect fit around a vertex. One common semiregular tessellation contains 2 hexagons and 2 equilateral triangles.

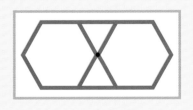

We looked at this tile pattern on page 12 when we were discussing hexagons and 6-pointed stars. As you can now see, the 6-pointed stars are formed by the turquoise triangular tiles that occur in each unit in the tessellation.

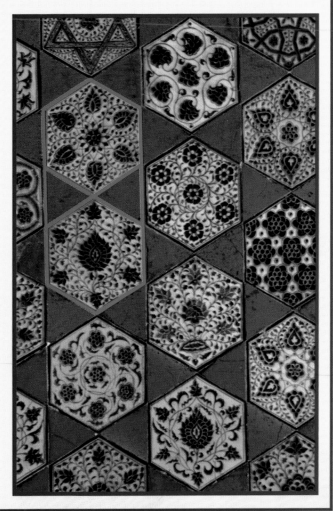

19

Another common semiregular tessellation contains 2 octagons and 1 square. Again, the 3 shapes meet to form a perfect fit around a vertex, and the angles around the vertex add up to 360°.

In the example below, the semiregular tessellation is formed by the designs painted on the tiles rather than by the shapes of the tiles themselves.

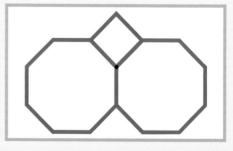

Tessellations can also be formed by more complex geometric shapes. Look at the carving shown below. The surface is covered by a semiregular tessellation made of two 6-pointed stars and 2 hexagons. Notice that the artist has transformed the hexagons and stars into flowers with 6 petals, thus combining geometric shapes with designs based on plant and flower forms.

This carving comes from the gateway to a mosque in Delhi, India, built in 1311.

Now imagine huge buildings covered with tessellations and patterns like those we have examined. The tessellations and patterns capture the viewer's attention. Everyday concerns and problems disappear, and the viewer contemplates the order and harmony expressed in the art. For Muslims, this is a powerful reminder of the order, balance, and unity in nature and the spiritual world.

Creating Your Own Geometric Designs

You can create your own geometric designs like those seen in Islamic art. You'll need a compass, a protractor, and a pencil. Let's get started!

Begin by creating a design with hexagons and 6-pointed stars. First, use your compass to draw a circle. Make a small mark at the top of the circle.

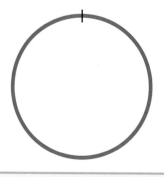

Using your protractor, make 6 marks on the **circumference** at 60-degree intervals, starting from the mark at the top (6 x 60° = 360°).

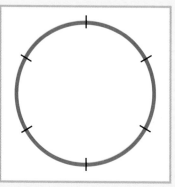

Draw straight lines to connect the marks on the circumference, as shown at the right. Use the straight edge of your protractor to help you. Now you have a hexagon inside a circle.

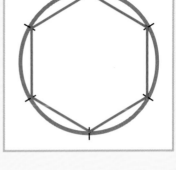

Starting at the top, draw straight lines to connect every second angle of the hexagon. Now you have an equilateral triangle inside the hexagon.

Draw straight lines to connect the other 3 angles of the hexagon. Now you have a second equilateral triangle. Together, the overlapping equilateral triangles form a 6-pointed star.

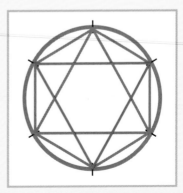

Draw straight lines to connect every second angle of the hexagon inside the star. Draw straight lines to connect the remaining 3 angles of the hexagon inside the star. Now you have another 6-pointed star.

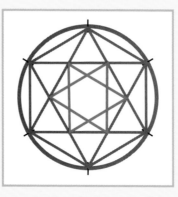

Repeat the above steps with the hexagon inside the second star. This will give you yet another 6-pointed star. We'll stop here, but you could go on and on doing this until the stars and hexagons were too small to see.

Now let's create a design with octagons and 8-pointed stars. Once again, start by using your compass to draw a circle.

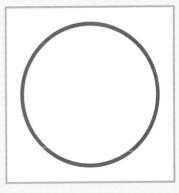

Using your protractor, make marks on the circumference at 90-degree intervals, placed as shown in the diagram.

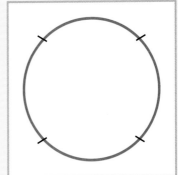

Draw straight lines to connect the marks on the circumference, as shown at the right. Use the straight edge of your protractor to help you. Now you have a square inside a circle.

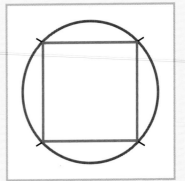

Locate the midpoint on each side of the square. Draw a mark on the circle's circumference at exactly that point.

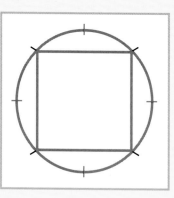

Draw straight lines to connect these marks. Now you have a second square. Together, the overlapping squares form an 8-pointed star.

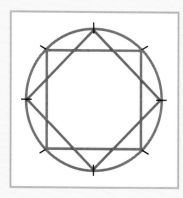

Draw straight lines to connect the points of the star. Now you have an octagon around your 8-pointed star.

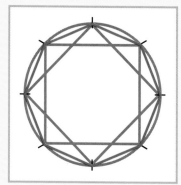

Instead of an octagon, you might want to create an 8-pointed star with longer points. Start with your drawing of an 8-pointed star, and extend the lines that form the sides of the first square.

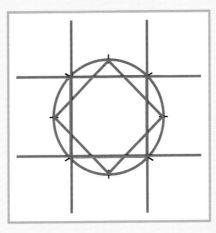

Now extend the lines that form the sides of the second square. You've created a new 8-pointed star with long points.

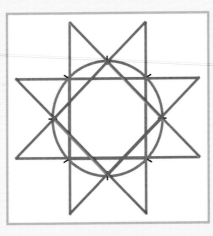

Now let's use interlocking circles to create a flower with 6 evenly spaced petals. Start by using your compass to draw a circle.

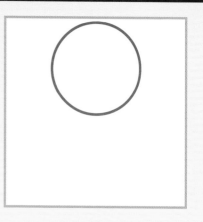

Next, place the point of your compass on the bottom of the circle's circumference and draw a second circle that is the same size as the first.

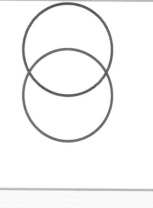

Place the point of your compass on the bottom of the second circle's circumference and draw a third circle that is the same size as the first and second circles.

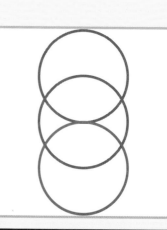

Place the point of your compass at the point where the first and second circles intersect on the left side (point A) and draw another circle. Then place the point of your compass at the point where the second and third circles intersect on the left side (point B) and draw another circle.

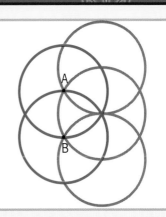

Repeat these steps on the right side. In the center, where the 7 circles intersect, is a flower with 6 evenly spaced petals.

If you want, you can create an extended pattern of flowers by continuing to draw circles that have their center at the point where 2 other circles intersect.

Now that you've learned how to make some of the geometric designs we've seen in Islamic art, try combining them. See if you can make a pattern or tessellation to cover a whole page.

Math and Meaning

You're probably used to thinking of math as a subject you study in school. You may also think of it as a tool that can help you solve practical problems. As you've learned in this book, however, math has a much deeper meaning for many people. It expresses principles that govern nature and the spiritual world. This is true not just for Muslims but for many other people as well. Circles may represent wholeness or community for Native Americans, for example. For Christians, Hindus, and Buddhists, the circle is a symbol for eternity, and the square represents the physical world. These 2 geometric shapes play important roles in Christian, Hindu, and Buddhist art.

Forms of math other than geometry may also have meaning for cultures. **Architects** of the Italian **Renaissance**, for example, developed theories about ideal ratios and proportions that they used to give harmony to their buildings. You can't see the math when you look at the buildings, but without it the buildings wouldn't have the effect that they do.

Now that you know something about the role math can play in art, look for it in paintings, buildings, signs, and posters around you. You may be surprised at what you find.

Glossary

architect (AR-kuh-tekt) Someone who designs buildings.

bilateral (by-LA-tuh-ruhl) Having 2 sides.

circumference (suhr-KUHM-fuh-ruhns) The perimeter of a circle.

diagram (DY-uh-gram) A drawing that shows the arrangement of something.

diversity (duh-VUHR-suh-tee) Variety.

equilateral triangle (ee-kwuh-LA-tuh-ruhl TRY-an-guhl) A triangle with all sides of equal length.

hexagon (HEK-suh-gahn) A shape with 6 angles and 6 sides.

interlock (IN-tuhr-lahk) To join or connect through shared parts.

intersect (in-tuhr-SEKT) To share a common area.

octagon (AHK-tuh-gahn) A shape with 8 angles and 8 sides.

overlap (oh-vuhr-LAP) To occupy the same area in part.

polygon (PAH-lee-gahn) A closed plane shape with straight sides.

Renaissance (reh-nuh-SAHNS) The name for the period in Italy from the 1300s to the late 1500s when there was a revival of ancient Greek and Roman art and architecture. The name comes from a French word that means "rebirth."

vertex (VUHR-teks) The common endpoint of the lines of an angle.

visual (VIH-zhuh-wuhl) Appealing to sight.

Index